Comprehension Success 2

James Driver

Oxford University Press

Preface

Comprehension is a comprehensive activity that involves many different aspects of English. This book uses the traditional role of comprehension – asking questions on the content of short texts – as a starting-point from which to investigate, in depth, a variety of different kinds of writing.

The thirty double-pages of comprehensions offer a wide variety of texts – examples from information books, action rhymes, realia such as postcards and notices, children's fiction, fable, catalogues, comic strips, picture books, poems and legends – a whole range of genres, drawn from authentic texts.

The pupils are then encouraged to use a range of strategies to discover meaning. They will practise locating, selecting, collating, identifying, using, retrieving, examining and re-presenting ideas and information, and, by employing quotation, deduction and inference, find that their confidence as readers who fully appreciate a text will continue to grow.

There are three sections on most of the question pages. Section A contains the most straightforward recall questions. The questions in Section B often call for a deeper insight into the nature of the text. The knowledge gained from answering one, or both, of these two sets of questions is used in Section C, which offers a prompt for a creative writing activity, in the same genre as the selected text.

The confidence that comes from being able to understand the main points about the facts, characters and events that appear in a broad range of texts encourages readers to read more widely and enables them to gain a better understanding of how writing, its form, language and content, works. This, in turn, should lead to a faster development of their ability as writers.

Oxford University Press, Great Clarendon Street, Oxford OX2 6DP

Oxford New York
Athens Auckland Bangkok Bogota Buenos Aires Calcutta
Cape Town Chennai Dar es Salaam Delhi Florence Hong Kong
Istanbul Karachi Kuala Lumpur Madrid Melbourne Mexico City
Mumbai Nairobi Paris São Paulo Singapore
Taipei Tokyo Toronto Warsaw

and associated companies in
Berlin Ibadan

Oxford is a trade mark of Oxford University Press

© Oxford University Press 1998
First published 1998
Reprinted 1998 (twice)

ISBN 0 19 834179 2

Typeset and designed by Oxprint Design, Oxford

Printed in China

Contents

A contents page

This contents page comes from the beginning of a magazine. It tells you about the different kinds of writing you will find in the magazine, and on which pages the different kinds of writing start.

1 What is the name of the story Princess Alice appears in?

2 What can you learn about on page 27?

3 Which page would you turn to if you wanted to **make** something?

4 What is the name of the dog that appears in the **last** story?

5 Which other story has a dog in it?

6 What kind of writing would you find on page 38?

The magazine is 50 pages long and has 6 different articles in it.

1 a) Which is the longest piece in the magazine?
  b) Which is the shortest piece in the magazine?

2 How often does this magazine come out?

3 Most of the articles in the magazine cover the same subject.
  What is that?

4 How can you tell that **Charlotte and Henry** appear in every issue of the magazine?

5 a) Which article in the magazine would **you** like to read most?
  b) Why would you choose this article?

Most of the different articles in the magazine are about the same subject.

1 Imagine you are in charge of making the **next** magazine. What subject would you like most of the articles to be about?

2 When you have decided on the subject, design a **Contents page** for the magazine. Try to include a short description of the **story**, a little piece about the **factfile**, something to **make**, a **game**, a **poem** and another episode in the adventures of **Charlotte and Henry**. Set your page out in the same style as the opposite page.

Glossary

This page is from the back of an information book. It reminds the reader about some of the words that have been used in that book.

Useful words

You can find all of these words in this book. The pictures will help you to remember what the words mean.

canal
This is a special waterway built for ships and to carry water across land.

condensation
This is tiny drops of water you see on cold things. It forms when warm, damp air touches something cold.

dam
This is a wall built to hold water back and make a lake.

desert
This is a dry place, where it hardly ever rains. Only a few plants grow.

dew
This is the name for the small drops of water which form on cool ground, leaves and plants.

evaporate
This is what happens when water dries up. It turns into tiny, invisible water drops in the air.

A

1 What topic do you think the book was about?

2 What do you call a place where it hardly ever rains?

3 What do you call the drops of water that form on cool plants?

4 Which word on the opposite page means a **man-made waterway**?

5 Why does a **dam** have to be strong?

6 When water **evaporates**, where does it go?

B

1 Why don't many plants grow in a desert?

2 Steam from a kettle touches a cold kitchen window.
   a) What will you see on the window?
   b) What is the correct word that describes what is happening?

3 Heavy rain falls on a school playground, making big puddles. The sun comes out. The puddles disappear. What has happened to the rainwater? Where has it gone?

4 You go camping in a farmer's field. You wake up early and go for a walk. It hasn't rained during the night but soon your shoes are soaking. What has made the grass so wet?

C

Now look up the words from this **glossary** in your classroom dictionary.

Write down how your dictionary describes the meaning of each word.

Which do you think is the better description for each?

How bread is made

The pictures and writing on these pages come from a book all about different kinds of fungi. When we think of fungi we usually think of mushrooms. *Yeast* doesn't look like a mushroom or a toadstool, but it is a type of fungus that is very useful.

yeast cells

Another useful fungus is called yeast. Yeast is used to make bread and to make beer. The picture shows tiny yeast cells. Yeast cells feed on sugar and on starch. As they feed, they give off a gas called carbon dioxide.

dough

1 What food is yeast used in?

2 What drink is yeast used in?

3 Name **two** things yeast cells feed on.

4 What comes out of yeast cells when they are feeding?

5 What do you call bread **before** it is cooked?

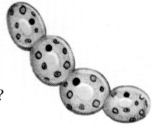

Bakers make dough for bread from flour,
sugar, milk and water.
There is a lot of starch in flour.
If the dough were cooked it would be flat
and hard.
But the baker adds yeast to the dough.
The yeast feeds on the sugar and starch,
and gives off bubbles of carbon dioxide.
These bubbles are trapped in the dough
and make it rise.
When it is cooked, the bread is soft
and light.

dough rises

bread baked

1 What would bread be like if it was made without any yeast?

2 Where does the yeast find the starch it needs to feed on?

3 What else does the baker give the yeast to feed on?

4 What does a baker let the dough do **before** it is cooked?

Now continue the text to tell how the bread gets from the baker
to your kitchen table.

What transport is involved, and what packing?

Horrible Aunt Pen

This is the beginning of a children's story by Janice Elliott, which describes the characters and the setting of the story.

Aunt Pen's black house was on a black cliff by a grey sea. She had no flowers in her garden, only concrete, so that the children should not pick the flowers. She had no friends, only a fierce cat. The cat was black and his name was Black Cat. While Christopher Magnifico and Aunt Pen ate dry bread and semolina, Black Cat ate fat silver fish, jellies, peanut-butter sandwiches, chips, steak-and-kidney pie and ice cream. When Christopher Magnifico arrived Aunt Pen said, as she always did: 'I don't know what I shall do with you. I do not know about boys. You had better go to bed.'

A

1 What is the name of the boy who comes to stay with Aunt Pen?

2 What is the name of Aunt Pen's cat?

3 What do you think is Aunt Pen's favourite colour?

4 List **three** things in the story that are Aunt Pen's favourite colour.

5 How can you tell that Aunt Pen's house looks out over the sea?

B

1 How can you tell that Aunt Pen liked her cat more than she liked the boy?

2 Write down the words that make it clear the boy had been there before.

3 Why does Aunt Pen send the boy to bed?

4 How can you tell Aunt Pen hated **all** children?

5 Which word does the writer use to describe the cat that tells you the cat is horrible too?

6 Look carefully at the picture. The artist has given the cat a treat the writer didn't put in the story. What is this extra treat?

C

Aunt Pen's cat has an amazing **menu** to choose from.

A **menu** is the list of food you can choose from when you go out to eat at a restaurant, a cafe, a hotel, or even in a school canteen!

1 Write out the **menu** you would like to choose from at lunchtime.

2 Write out the **menu** you think a **lion** would like to choose from.

3 Write out the **menu** a **monster**, like a **vampire**, would like.

4 Write out the **menu** a **spider** would like to choose from.

Mrs Mather

This is a poem by a well-known children's poet, which ends with a terrible question.

MRS MATHER

Scared stiff.
Courage flown.
On that doorstep all alone.
Cold sweat.
State of shock.
Lift my trembling hand and knock.

Thumping heart.
Chilled with fear.
I hear the witch's feet draw near.
Rasping bolts.
Rusty locks.
Shake down to my cotton socks.

Hinges creaking.
Waft of mould.
A groan that makes my blood run cold.
Cracking voice.
Knocking knees.
"Can I have my ball back, please?"

Colin McNaughton

A

1 Where is the boy standing?

2 How is the boy feeling?

3 What is he going to do with his trembling hand?

4 What is the name of the woman who lives in the house?

5 Write down **two** things the woman has used to fasten her door.

6 What noise does the door make when it opens?

7 What noise does the woman make when she sees the boy?

8 What does the boy ask the woman who lives in the house?

B

1 Why do you think the poet starts with 'scared stiff' on a line by itself?

2 What can the boy smell when the door opens?

3 Which word does the poet rhyme with 'knees'?

4 What does the boy feel on his face that shows he is frightened?

5 How can a voice 'crack' ?

C

In many of the lines in the poem the poet has used short **phrases** – two or three words together – to describe how scared the boy is feeling.

'Scared stiff' 'Thumping heart' 'Cracking voice' 'Knocking knees'

Imagine you wake up in the middle of the night and see an alien spacecraft hovering outside your window. The door of the craft is opening slowly ...

Write a poem about how you feel, using short phrases as in the poem opposite.

Tail to tail

This page comes from a book that is full of picture puzzles.

1 a) What is the sun doing?

 b) Turn the page upside down. Now what is the sun doing?

2 Find the hare and the ram, then make a **list** of the four other **real** animals that appear in the picture.

3 What does the horse with the dog's legs have on its back?

1 When the hare gets mixed up with the ram you might call the new animal a **ham**! It is possible to make some more real words from some other mixes.
 a) What could you call the ram when it is mixed up with the cat?
 b) What could you call the cow when it is mixed up with the hare?
 c) What could you call the horse when it is mixed up with the dog?

2 Look around the edges of the picture. Use the five **red** letters to make a word that describes what you do when you are happy.

3 Two words round the edge **sound** the same, but mean something different. Find those words and write down what they mean. (If you are not sure you can use a dictionary.)

1 Make a **list** of all the mixed up animals.

2 Chose your **three** favourite mixed up animals.

3 Imagine these three animals have a race.

They race across the countryside that is in the picture at the **top** of the page.

They start at the castle on the right and finish at the little gate on the left.

You are the televison **commentator** for the race.

Write down what you say during the race.

Different parts of the race course will suit different animals. The horse's legs will go fast in the grass fields. The cat's paws will be useful for climbing trees and fences. A dog's sharp eyes will be useful for finding hidden paths.

Who is going to win?

Moles

This is a page from an information book, with labels adding more facts to the illustration.

Life underground

Some places are covered with grass but don't have many trees or bushes. There are not many places for animals to hide in these grasslands. Many small animals live underground to keep safe from their enemies.

Moles

Moles spend nearly all their life underground. They can dig fast with their large front feet. They feed on the earthworms they catch as they dig through the soil.

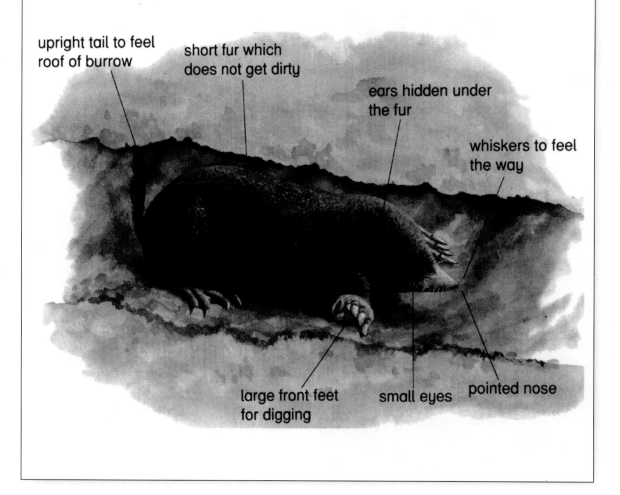

upright tail to feel roof of burrow

short fur which does not get dirty

ears hidden under the fur

whiskers to feel the way

large front feet for digging

small eyes

pointed nose

A

1 What do moles eat?

2 Why is it quite unusual to see a mole?

3 What would happen to a mole if it had long, thick hair on its body?

4 Why does the mole have such large front feet?

5 Why do you think moles have their ears hidden under their fur?

B

1 Apart from the fact that their food lives underground, why do moles spend most of their lives beneath the surface?

2 **a)** What part of their bodies do moles use to discover what is front of them?

   b) What part of their bodies do moles use to discover what is above them?

3 **a)** Find a word that is used in the piece of writing about moles that is the **opposite** of **clean**.

   b) Find a word that is used in the piece of writing about moles that means the **same** as **tunnel**.

C

A group of scientists decide they want to study moles. They decide to make a safe, outdoor, mole enclosure. From above it must still look like part of the grasslands but it must also be designed in such a way that the scientists can see the moles as they go about their everyday activities.

So that the moles are safe the mole enclosure must be able to keep out dogs, foxes, cats and hawks.

1 Draw a **picture** of your mole enclosure.

2 Write **labels** to point out its best features.

3 Make a **list** of all the materials and tools you will need to make it.

Tropical rainforest

This is a factual description of a tropical rainforest. Because of the climate rainforests are full of many different plants and animals.

Plants are everywhere. Mosses, ferns, flowers and trees are all crowded together with hardly a space between. This is a tropical rain forest, warm and dripping with water. Heavy rain showers soak everything, making it easy for plants to draw up water through their roots. In dry places such as deserts, plants and animals have had to develop ways to store water. In a rain forest, where there is plenty of water and food, animals such as the crocodile find life much easier.

A

1 Name **two** types of plant that grow in the rainforest.

2 Which part of a plant collects water from the ground?

3 Why don't rainforest plants need to store water?

4 How is a **desert** different from a **rainforest**?

B

1 Fill in the missing letters in this sentence, then copy it down:
'Rainforests are **w** _ _ _ and **w** _ _.'

2 Write down the word in the passage that means **make wet**.

3 Write down the phrase in the passage that means **close together**.

4 Why do so many plants grow in rainforests?

5 Crocodiles don't eat plants. Why is there plenty of food for crocodiles to eat in the rainforest?

C

Look carefully at the picture.

1 Why do you think the crocodile is the same colour as the mud, the water and the leaves of the rainforest plants?

2 If the crocodile was floating in the river, keeping very still, what do you think it might look like?

3 Imagine your class goes on an expedition to the rainforest.

You are put in charge of **safety**.

So that no-one in your class is eaten by a crocodile write out a list of **instructions** that explain clearly what they must do when they are in, on and by the river.

You could use these words as starting points:

Don't .... Look out for .... Remember ....

Trail-blazing

These diagrams are from a book on how to survive if you are lost in a dangerous place.

A

1 How many bunches of grass are used in the **Danger** sign?

2 How many sticks are used in the **Danger** sign?

3 How many sticks are used in the **Turn to the right** sign?

4 What do you have to do to the grass before you make a sign with it?

5 What would you do if you found three upright sticks in your path?

6 What is the difference between the stone sign for **Danger** and the stone sign for **This is the road**?

7 a) Which material – grass, stone or stick – do you think would be the most difficult to make signs out of?

   b) Why do you think it would be so hard to make signs out of this material?

B

1 a) Which signs might be useless if it was very windy?

   b) How would these signs be affected by a strong wind?

2 Why do you think the diagram shows three different kinds of materials?

3 What would you do to the stick sign for **Danger** if you wanted to make someone following the trail think that they were on the right road?

4 a) Which material – stone, stick or grass – would you like to use if you were setting a trail?

   b) Why would you choose this material?

C

Here is an extract from an explorer's **diary**. The explorer was leaving a trail for the rest of the expedition to follow. Copy it out, and as you do so whenever you think the explorer ought to have left a sign **draw** the correct sign onto your page.

MONDAY.

Set off early across the grasslands. Came to a crossroads. Chose the path through the wood to the right. Walked for a mile along a stony track. Saw a track to the left. Didn't take it. Suddenly found I was standing under a huge wild bees' nest! Ran to the river. Followed the bank to the left. Found two bridges. The stone bridge was wobbly. Went on the wooden one. Saw a tiger!

Town plan

This map comes from a local guidebook, to help visitors know where to park.

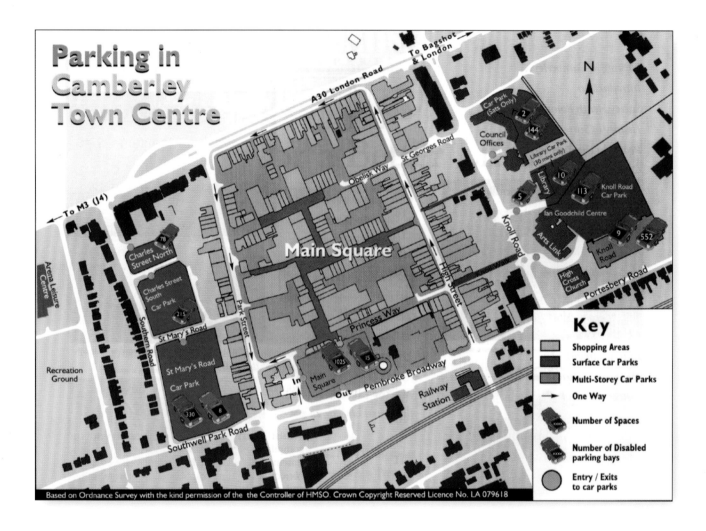

A

1 Can you think of **two** groups of people who would find this map very useful?

2 Write down the name of the car park that can hold the most cars.

3 Write down the name of a car park that **doesn't** have special spaces for disabled drivers.

4 Which car park should a disabled driver use to go to the shops in Park Street?

5 When you drive **out** of the Main Square multi-storey car park, which road do you find yourself in?

B

1 You don't have to come in your car to go shopping in Camberley. What other form of transport can you use?

2 **a)** Which car park do you think the shoppers like best?
   b) Why do you think the shoppers like this car park best?

3 Why do you think the car park by the Council Offices is not open on Monday, Tuesday, Wednesday, Thursday and Friday?

4 How many cars do you think can be parked in **all** the car parks in Camberley on a Saturday? Do you think it is:

   3506 2506 1506 506 or 56 ?

C

Maps help people to find their way about the place.
Maps need to be clearly drawn and easy to read. They need to have clear labels so that you can tell exactly where you are. Look carefully at the map of Camberley Town Centre. Notice how the roads and car parks are clearly marked and how the key gives you plenty of information.

1 Draw a map, with clear labels, that shows a visitor to your school how to get to your classroom.

2 Invent an island of your own. Draw a map of the island. Use clear labels to show where the streams are, where an explorer will find jungle, rocky cliffs, dangerous swamps, strange creatures, haunted ruins, sea monsters, hidden villages, mysterious messages, food and buried treasure.

   Don't forget to include a **key** that explains all the symbols you have used.

From fireplace to flap

This is a page from the *Oxford Illustrated Junior Dictionary*, which gives you meanings of words, and their parts of speech.

fireplace *noun* **fireplaces**
the part of a room where you can have a fire.

firework *noun* **fireworks**
a thing that burns or explodes with loud bangs and coloured lights.

firm *adjective* **firmer, firmest**
something that is firm is hard and does not move easily. *That shelf is not very firm so don't put too many books on it.*
firmly *adverb*

first *adjective, adverb*
before all others.
A is the first letter of the alphabet.
I came first in the race.

first aid *noun*
help that you give to a person who is hurt, before a doctor comes.

fish *noun* **(fishes** or **fish)**
any animal with scales and fins that lives and breathes in water.

fish *verb* **fishes, fishing, fished**
to try to catch fish.

fisherman *noun* **fishermen**
a person who tries to catch fish.

fist *noun* **fists**
a tightly-closed hand.

fit *adjective* **fitter, fittest**
1 healthy, strong. *Swimming helps to keep you fit.*
2 good enough. *Is this old bread fit to eat?*

fit *verb* **fits, fitting, fitted**
to be the right size and shape. *These jeans don't fit me anymore.*

five *noun* **fives**
the number 5.
fifth *adjective*

fix *verb* **fixes, fixing, fixed**
1 to join firmly to something.
Fix the shelf onto the wall.
2 to mend.
She fixed the broken toy.

fizzy *adjective* **fizzier, fizziest**
with a lot of tiny bubbles that keep bursting.
fizzy drinks.

flag *noun* **flags**
a piece of cloth, often with a coloured design on it, used as a sign or signal.
Every country has its own flag.

Union Flag
Scotland
China
United States
Australia
New Zealand
Italy
Wales
Eire
Pakistan
India
Barbados
Japan
Germany
France

flame *noun* **flames**
fire shaped like a pointed tongue. *a candle flame.*

flannel *noun* **flannels**
a piece of soft cloth used for washing yourself.

flap *noun* **flaps**
a flat piece of something joined along one edge so that it covers an opening.
The flap of an envelope.

73

a b c d e **f** g h i j k l m n o p q r s t u v w x y z

To fill the gaps in the sentences choose words from the dictionary page.
Make sure you don't use the same word more than once.
When you have chosen a word to fill each gap, write down the sentence.

1 I heard a _____ make a great bang as it lit up the sky.

2 The _____ was full of paper, wood and coal.

3 I could tell the drink was _____ because it was bubbling.

4 If you want to _____ the door you will need a screwdriver.

5 The _____ from the match lit the rocket.

6 The _____ held the tiny fish in his _____ .

7 If the pole stays _____ the _____will be seen.

8 The _____was so _____ it easily leapt up the waterfall.

Look at the pictures of the flags.

1 Write down the names of **two** countries that have little Union Jacks as part of their flags.

2 Write down the names of **two** countries that have red and white stripes in their flags.

3 How is the flag of Italy different from the flag of France?

4 Several of the flags have stars as part of their design.
   a) Which country has the moon on its flag?
   b) Which country shows the sun on its flag as a simple, round shape?

5 a) Which flag do you think has the most eye-catching design?
   b) Why did you choose this flag?

The shapes that appear on flags often have special meanings. The flag for Barbados has a trident – a three-pronged spear used for catching fish – because Barbados is an island where many of the people are fishermen. On the flag of the United States there is a tiny star for each of the different states – like California and Texas – that make up the country.

Design a flag for your class. Make sure you choose shapes and colours that have special meanings for the people in your class. Make it as eye-catching as possible.

British & American English

This page is from an information book on facts of all kinds.

British and American English

Familiar things with different names

British	American	British	American
autumn	fall	pavement	sidewalk
biscuit	cookie	petrol	gasoline
bonnet (of car)	hood	post	mail
dustbin	garbage can	pushchair	stroller
holiday	vacation	queue	line
lift	elevator	railway	railroad
lorry	truck	rubber	eraser
motor car	automobile	sweets	candy
nappy	diaper	tap	faucet

The same word with different meanings

	British	American
homely	warm and friendly	plain and dull, or even ugly
mean	stingy	nasty
nervy	nervous	cheeky
pants	underpants	trousers
public school	private fee-paying	ordinary

Different spellings

British	American	British	American
analyse	analyze	mould	mold
catalogue	catalog	pyjamas	pajamas
colour	color	sulphur	sulfur
defence	defense	theatre	theater

English as a language is spoken in many countries all around the world. This page compares some meanings in Britain and America.

1 What time of year would it be described as in Britain if an American said it was 'the fall'?

2 Where would you go if an American asked you to 'Turn on the faucet'?

3 When would you put an American baby in a 'stroller'?

4 American babies wear 'diapers.' What are these called in Britain?

5 Where would you find a 'hood' on an American car?

6 How would an American use an 'eraser'?

1 Why would an American be surprised if a British person said they were wearing a pair of 'pants' under their trousers?

2 a) If you told an American teacher you were always 'nervy' at school, would the teacher be kind to you, or be cross with you?
   b) Why would the American teacher act this way?

3 If an American told you to keep on the 'sidewalk' to reach the 'gasoline' station, where would you be going, and how would you get there?

4 a) Would you prefer to live in a 'homely' house in Britain or a 'homely' house in America?
   b) Why did you make this choice?

These sentences have been written down by an American. Change them into the sentences that a British person would write. Don't forget you might have to change some of the spellings as well as the words.

1 When I was on vacation I went in an automobile to the theater.

2 The color catalog that came through the mail had pictures of pants, pajamas and lots of boxes of candy.

3 I was in the line for the elevator when I noticed mold on the cookie I was eating.

Personal data

This page is from an information book on exploring science.

What about us?

Look at these children. What can you see that is similar and different? Some things are obvious, others are not!

2 m
1.50 m
1 m
0.50 m

We have recorded some of their personal facts on this chart...

	GIRL?	BLUE EYES?	BROWN HAIR?	SWIM 200 m?	HAS A PET?	RIGHT HANDED?	TALLER THAN 1.50 m?
Ann	✓		✓				
Jim						✓	✓
Pete		✓				✓	
Angus				✓		✓	✓
Lyn	✓		✓	✓	✓		
							✓

PERSONAL DATA is another phrase for information about ourselves. There is a better way to store this DATA so that we can read it more quickly. We need some cards made like this...

Punch a hole by each statement.

Cut off corner so you can see that cards always face the same way.

GIRL
BLUE EYES
BROWN HAIR
SWIM 200 m
HAS A PET
RIGHT HANDED
TALLER THAN 1.50 m

Name.................

Not only do identical twins look alike but they often feel alike. When one twin is ill or injured the other will sometimes feel the pain!

Data is another word for information. If you collect data about people you are gathering information about them. On the opposite page some children have recorded data about others in the class.

1 How many children have had facts recorded about them?

2 How many of the children are girls?

3 How many of the children can swim 200 metres?

4 How many of the children are left-handed?

5 How many of the children are shorter than 1.50m?

6 a) Who is the only one who has a pet?

   b) Look closely at the line of children. What sort of pet is it?

1 What is the name of the boy wearing red trousers?

2 What is the name of the girl wearing the green skirt?

3 Who is raising both his hands in the air?

4 Write down **two** ways Ann is different from Lyn.

5 Write down **three** things Angus has in common with Pete.

6 Write down **two** things Jim has in common with Pete.

The **data card** on the opposite page carries a lot of information. It has seven different facts and the person's name.

Make a **data card** of your own like the one on the opposite page.

It must have a space for your name and must carry **nine** different facts about you!

If you like you can also draw a picture of yourself on your **data** card.

School timetable

This is the timetable for class 3JP. Their teacher is called Miss Parkinson. She teaches most of their lessons, but 3JP are also taught by some other teachers.

TIMETABLE

	B	1	2	3	B	4	5	L	6	7
M		Maths		P.E. (indoors) Mrs. Brown		Design and Technology Mr. Broadhurst			Quiet Reading	Music Miss Ward
T		Maths	Science Mr. Broadhurst			English	I.T.		ART Miss Ward	
W		English	Music Miss Ward			Maths	French Ms. Smith		History Topic (Romans in Britain)	
T		Maths	I.T.			Science Mr. Broadhurst			Geography Topic (Rivers)	
F		English	Pottery Mrs. Shukla			Science Mr. Broadhurst			P.E. (Outdoors)	

1 What lesson do 3JP have first on Wednesday morning?

2 What lesson do 3JP have last on a Monday?

3 What lesson do 3JP have after lunch on Tuesday?

4 As part of their P.E. lessons 3JP do dance in the Hall. What is the name of their dance teacher?

5 On which day should 3JP bring in their outdoor trainers?

6 On which day should Miss Parkinson bring in her collection of Roman coins?

7 Mr. Broadhurst teaches two different subjects; what are they?

8 a) How many different subjects does Miss Ward teach?
b) What are they?

9 3JP have two special lessons. They only have one of these lessons each week. What are these **two** special lessons?

10 Why might 3JP have a class trip to the River Thames?

1 a) If you were in 3JP which day of the school week would be your favourite day?
b) Write down **two** reasons why you think you would like this day better than the rest.

2 a) Which teacher do you think has the most enjoyable job?
b) Why do you think this teacher has the best job?

Copy down the grid from the opposite page, but leave all the lessons blank. When you have finished write down **your** perfect week. When you have chosen all the things you like to do best, write down the people you would like to teach these things to you. They don't have to be your real teachers. You might like a famous athlete to come in and teach you P.E. You might like your favourite singer to teach your class music. You might like to use a Time Machine to bring back people from the past to teach you history!

Telling the time

There are many different ways of telling the time. Here is a page from an encyclopedia that gives you pictures of two different types of time-tellers: watches and sundials.

 ## Clocks and watches

The ancient Egyptians used water clocks to measure time. Mechanical clocks and watches, with an hour hand and a minute hand, were not made until the 17th century. Atomic clocks are the world's most accurate timekeepers. They are accurate to within one second in 1·6 million years.

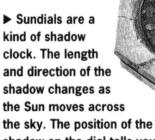
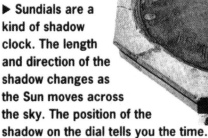

▶ Sundials are a kind of shadow clock. The length and direction of the shadow changes as the Sun moves across the sky. The position of the shadow on the dial tells you the time.

▼ An analogue watch uses hands and a dial to show the time. When you look at the hands, it is easy to see that there are 15 minutes to go before four o'clock.

▼ A digital watch uses numbers to show the time. It keeps time very accurately, but you cannot see at a glance how long it is until four o'clock. You have to work it out for yourself.

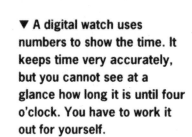

▲ Lots of modern watches are brightly coloured and inexpensive. They use the natural vibrations (100,000 times per second) in a quartz crystal to keep time, and their power comes from tiny batteries.

A

1 What points to the time on a sundial?

2 What points to the time on an analogue watch?

3 What shows the time on a digital watch?

4 What powers a quartz crystal watch?

5 Why are watches more useful than sundials?

B

1 Apart from the fact they both tell the time, how is an analogue watch similar to a sundial?

2 Why does the shadow on a sundial move across the dial?

3 a) If you were timing the runners in a race would you prefer to use a digital watch, an analogue watch or a sundial?

   b) Why do you think this time-keeper would be the best for the job?

4 a) There are four different types of timekeepers pictured on the opposite page. Which one would you like to own?

   b) Why do you prefer this one to the others?

5 a) Which of the timekeepers on the opposite page do you think was invented first?

   b) Explain why you think this was the first to be made.

C

Imagine you are in charge of a Clock and Watch Museum. One of your jobs is to write the **labels** for all the different objects you have on display. The labels are not very big; they only have room for **20** words.

1 Write a **label** for a sundial explaining, in **20** words or less, what it is and how it tells the time.

2 Write a **label** for an analogue watch explaining, in 20 words or less, what it is and how it tells the time.

3 Write a **label** for a digital watch explaining, in 20 words or less, what it is and how it tells the time.

Television

This information comes from a brochure produced by a new television channel.

There are three ways that television can be sent to your home. The first is when the TV station **transmits** radio waves which are picked up by your TV aerial.

The second way we receive television is by **satellite**. The TV station sends the programme up to a satellite in space. The satellite then sends the programme back to earth. To receive satellite programmes, you need a satellite dish.

Television is also transmitted by **cable**. In some areas, electrical cables have been laid along the streets and into homes.

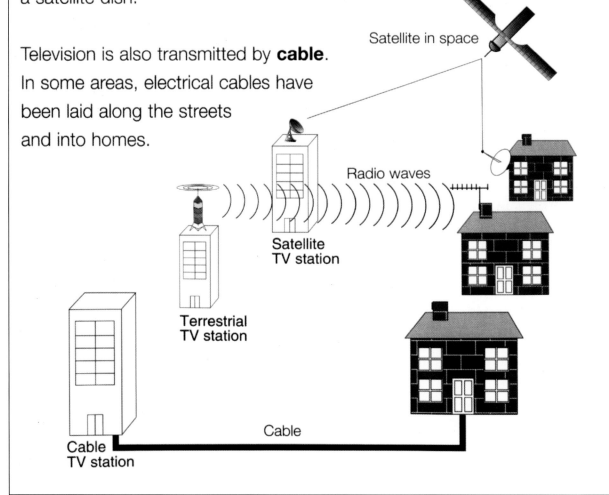

A

1 How many ways can TV stations send television to people's homes?

2 If the television programmes are sent by **radio waves** what do you have to have connected to your TV?

3 If the television programmes are sent by **satellite** what do you need to have on your house?

4 Why don't houses that have **cable** television need a receiver on their house or on their roof?

B

1 What is the word used on the opposite page that means **sends**?

2 **a)** If you lived in a house in a very windy part of the world, which way of receiving television programmes would you choose?
   b) Why do you think this would be the best method?

3 **a)** Which way of transmitting television do you think would be best for sending a televison programme to a country on the other side of the world?
   b) Explain why you have chosen this method.

C

You are in charge of setting up a new TV channel.

What programmes will you choose to transmit at different times of day?

Make up one day of programmes, and say who will enjoy each programme on your schedule.

A book of nonsense

These poems are all called limericks, and were written and illustrated by Edward Lear.

There was an Old Person of Sparta,
Who had twenty-five sons and one daughter;
　　He fed them on snails,
　　And weighed them in scales,
That wonderful Person of Sparta.

There was an Old Person of Dover,
Who rushed through a field of blue Clover:
　　But some very large bees
　　Stung his nose and his knees,
So he very soon went back to Dover.

There was an Old Man who said, "Hush!
I perceive a young bird in this bush!"
　　When they said, "Is it small?"
　　He replied, "Not at all!
It is four times as big as the bush!"

There was a Young Lady of Troy,
Whom several large flies did annoy;
　　Some she killed with a thump,
　　Some she drowned at the pump,
And some she took with her to Troy.

There was an Old Man who supposed,
That the street door was partially closed;
　　But some very large rats
　　Ate his coats and his hats,
While that futile old gentleman dozed.

A

1 How many children did the Old Person of Sparta have?

2 What did the Old Person of Sparta feed his children on?

3 What was the colour of the flowers that had attracted the bees?

4 Why did the Old Person go back to Dover?

5 What was unusual about the bird the Old Man found in the bush?

6 What do you notice about the picture the artist has drawn of the Old Man who finds the strange bird in the bush?

7 What did the Young Lady of Troy do with the water from the pump?

8 What came through the Old Man's door?

9 What happened to the Old Man's clothes?

B

1 Write down the word that appears in the limerick about the Old Man and the rats that means **slightly**.

2 Write down the word that appears in the limerick about the Old Man and the rats that means **useless**.

3 **a)** Which **one** of the characters that appears in these limericks would you like to hear more about?

   b) Explain why you want to discover more about this person.

4 **a)** Which **one** of the characters that appears in these limericks would you **not** like to meet?

   b) Explain why you do **not** want to meet him or her.

C

Look at how the **limericks** are written. Read them softly to yourself and feel the rhythm. Count the number of beats in each line.

A **limerick** has 5 lines.

The first line rhymes with the second line **and** the fifth line.

The third line rhymes only with the fourth line.

Write your own limerick that begins:

There was a small child in our school

(Don't forget to put the right number of the beats in each line!)

Adventures of Isabel

Ogden Nash was famous for writing poems with lively rhythm, and wonderful rhyming words.

Adventures of Isabel

Isabel met an enormous bear,
Isabel, Isabel, didn't care;
The bear was hungry, the bear was ravenous,
The bear's big mouth was cruel and cavernous.
The bear said, Isabel, glad to meet you,
How do, Isabel, now I'll eat you!
Isabel, Isabel, didn't worry,
Isabel didn't scream or scurry.
She washed her hands and she straightened her hair up,
Then Isabel quietly ate the bear up.

Once in a night as black as pitch
Isabel met a wicked old witch.
The witch's face was cross and wrinkled,
The witch's gums with teeth were sprinkled.
Ho ho, Isabel! the old witch crowed,
I'll turn you into an ugly toad!
Isabel, Isabel, didn't worry,
Isabel didn't scream or scurry.
She showed no rage and she showed no rancor,
But she turned the witch into milk and drank her.

Ogden Nash

A

1 Why was the bear pleased to see Isabel?

2 How can you tell that Isabel wasn't frightened by the bear?

3 What did Isabel do to the bear?

4 What did the witch say she was going to do to Isabel?

5 How did Isabel get rid of the witch?

B

1 Write down the rhymes at the end of lines that are spelt the same way.

2 Write down the rhymes at the end of lines that are spelt differently.

3 Write down the rhymes where two words rhyme at the end of the lines.

4 Write down the rhymes where one word rhymes with two words.

5 Write down the two lines that repeat as a chorus in both verses of the poem.

6 In the picture there is a cave on the top of the hill. It looks rather like the bear's mouth. The poet uses a word that has the word 'cave' in it to describe the bear's mouth. Write this word down.

C

At the start of the second verse the poet tells us the night was **'as black as pitch'**. 'Pitch' is another word for the tar that is used to make roads, so the poet is telling us that the night was very dull and dark. In these sentences the last word has been missed out. Fill the gaps by choosing the best word from the list on the right.

1 Isabel was as quiet as a _____

2 The bear was as big as a _____

3 The witch sounded like an old _____

4 The flowers were as white as _____

| enormous |
| house |
| mouse |
| crow |
| mole |
| snow |
| fireworks |

A Russian mystery

This is part of a true story about the children of the Russian royal family in 1917, who were being held as prisoners.

One day, Anastasia and Alexis decided to build an 'ice-mountain'. They carried water from the kitchen and poured it over a mound of snow, where it froze. They had to run with their buckets, for water became ice almost at once in the cold air. Everyone joined in, and the ice became so high that Anastasia and her brother were able to take sledge rides from the top. The older sisters could not resist the fun, and soon they were all laughing and tumbling in the snow. It was very disappointing when the guards decided that the ice-mountain was too high and must be destroyed.

A

1 What did the children use to carry the water?

2 What did they pour the water over?

3 How can you tell it was **very** cold?

4 Why did the children want to make the ice mountain so high?

5 Look at the picture. What other game did the childen play?

B

1 Look at the picture. How many older sisters did Anastasia have?

2 How can you tell the children were prisoners?

3 Why did the people in charge of the children say the ice mountain had to be destroyed?

4 Why do **you** think the people in charge of the children ordered the ice mountain to be destroyed?

5 If Anastasia had managed to escape, do you think she could have remained free without being re-discovered?

C

Imagine you are one of the children in the picture.

You are being kept prisoner.

It is very cold. It has snowed. You have a sledge. One guard is keeping warm in the kitchen. The other guard is at the bottom of the ice mountain.

You decide to escape!

Make an escape **plan**.

Your escape **plan** must have a **list** of all the things you are going to take with you so that you won't die in the snow.

Your escape **plan** must have **instructions** telling the rest of your family what they must do when you try to escape.

You might like to add a **map** showing where the guards are, where the ice mountain is, where the kitchen is, and which way you are going to go.

Big Jim

This is the *second* chapter of a book. It tells the story of a boy who goes to stay for the summer holidays with his uncle. In this chapter the boy has just come back from the beach where he has met another boy who has been showing off and being nasty.

2 Big Jim

"Have you had a good day?"
Bob's uncle asked him, at supper.
"Well, not really," Bob admitted.
Then he told his uncle about Ken.

"Oh, he's just a big show-off,"
said his uncle, filling a glass.
"Take no notice of him.
Still, it's quite a time
since you had that operation.
Swimming would do you good.
If you're scared of deep water,
why not get Big Jim to give you
some proper swimming lessons?"

"Who's Big Jim?" Bob asked.
"You've met him already —
he's the chief beachguard,"
Bob's uncle said, smiling.
"Go and see him tomorrow."

He reached for the pudding
and knocked over his glass.
"Yeow!" he yelled, jumping up
as the water ran into his lap.
"You're not the only one
who has trouble with this stuff!"

A

1 Who is Bob staying with?

2 Who had spoilt Bob's day?

3 What was Big Jim's real job?

4 What did Bob's uncle want Big Jim to do?

5 What was Bob frightened of?

6 What meal is Bob eating in the picture?

B

1 What was Bob recovering from?

2 Where had Bob spent the day?

3 How does Bob's uncle have trouble with water?

4 Find a word on the opposite page that means **shouted**.

5 **a)** Look at the picture. What job do you think Bob's uncle once did?
   b) What clues make you think Bob's uncle did this job?

C

This page is only **part** of a story.

What do you think happened **before** this chapter?

What do you think will happen **after** this chapter?

1 How do you think Ken had showed off to Bob?

2 What do you think will happen when Big Jim gives Bob swimming lessons?

3 What do you think Bob will do when Ken tries to show off again?

4 Write out how you think the story will end.

Ruby

This is a complete funny story by Florence Parry Heide.

Ruby

Ruby wanted to go over to Ethel's house to play. But Ruby's mother said, 'You have to watch Clyde.'

Clyde was Ruby's baby brother. He had just learned to walk.

'I don't want to watch Clyde. I want to go over to Ethel's house to play,' said Ruby.

Ruby's mother was tired. She had been watching Clyde all day. 'You have to watch Clyde because I have to take a bubble bath,' said Ruby's mother. She went into the bathroom.

Ruby called Ethel. 'I'll be over in a minute.'

Then Ruby watched Clyde.

She watched him take all of the clothes out of every chest of drawers in all of the rooms.

She watched him take all of the rice and all of the flour and all of the salt and all of the sugar and all of the coffee out of all of the kitchen cupboards and spill it all on the nice clean floor.

She watched him pull the tablecloth off the kitchen table. The bananas that had been on the table landed on Clyde's head.

Ruby watched Clyde start to cry very loud.

Her mother came out of the bathroom.

'What's going on?' she asked. 'I told you to watch Clyde.'

'I was watching him,' said Ruby truthfully. 'I was watching him the whole time.'

In a few minutes Ruby was ringing Ethel's doorbell. 'I told you I'd be over in a minute,' she said. 'I just had to watch Clyde.'

A

1 What was the name of Clyde's sister?

2 Where did Ruby want to go and what did she want to do there?

3 How was Clyde's mother planning to relax?

4 Why did Clyde's mother need to relax?

5 What made Clyde's mother leave the bathroom?

6 What made Clyde so upset?

7 At the start of the story who was looking after Clyde?

8 At the end of the story who was looking after Clyde?

9 **a)** Who do you think should have been looking after Clyde at the end of the story?

   b) Explain why you chose this person.

B

1 What did Ruby's mother mean by 'watch'?

2 **a)** What did Ruby do when her mother asked her to watch Clyde?
   b) Why do you think Ruby behaved like this?

3 What extra work did Clyde make for the people who lived in the house?

4 **a)** At the end of the story would you have allowed Ruby to go out or would you have made her stay in?
   b) Why would you have treated her in this way?

5 Write down the sentence from the story that shows that Ruby knew her plan would work **before** she started to 'watch' Clyde.

6 **a)** If you were Ethel would you like to have Ruby as a friend?
   b) Why would you feel this way?

7 Was Clyde ever in danger? If you think he was, explain when he was at risk and what was putting him into danger.

C

Write a set of **instructions** that explain exactly what you would have to do if you were told to look after Clyde.

A lion in the meadow

This is a complete story by Margaret Mahy.

The little boy said, 'Mother, there is a lion in the meadow.'

The mother said, 'Nonsense, little boy.'

The little boy said, 'Mother, there is a big yellow lion in the meadow.'

The mother said, 'Nonsense, little boy.'

The little boy said, 'Mother, there is a big, roaring, yellow, whiskery lion in the meadow!'

The mother said, 'Little boy, you are making up stories again. There is nothing in the meadow but grass and trees. Go into the meadow and see for yourself.'

The little boy said, 'Mother, I'm scared to go into the meadow, because of the lion which is there.'

The mother said, 'Little boy, you are making up stories — so I will make up a story, too. . . . Do you see this match box? Take it out into the meadow and open it. In it will be a tiny dragon. The tiny dragon will grow into a big dragon. It will chase the lion away.'

The little boy took the match box and went away. The mother went on peeling the potatoes.

Suddenly the door opened.

In rushed a big, roaring, yellow, whiskery lion.

'Hide me!' it said. 'A dragon is after me!'

The lion hid in the broom cupboard.

Then the little boy came running in.

'Mother,' he said. 'That dragon grew too big. There is no lion in the meadow now. There is a DRAGON in the meadow.'

The little boy hid in the broom cupboard too.

'You should have left me alone,' said the lion. 'I eat only apples.'

'But there wasn't a real dragon,' said the mother. 'It was just a story I made up.'

'It turned out to be true after all,' said the little boy. 'You should have looked in the match box first.'

'That is how it is,' said the lion. 'Some stories are true, and some aren't. . . . But I have an idea. We will go and play in the meadow on the other side of the house. There is no dragon there.'

'I am glad we are friends now,' said the little boy.

The little boy and the big roaring yellow whiskery lion went to play in the other meadow. The dragon stayed where he was, and nobody minded.

The mother never ever made up a story again.

A

1 What did the little boy say was in the meadow?

2 What did his mother say was in the meadow?

3 What was the boy's mother doing while she was talking to her son?

4 What did the boy's mother say was in the matchbox?

5 Where did the lion hide?

6 Why wouldn't the lion have eaten the boy?

7 Why do you think the boy came running in after the lion?

8 Where did the little boy hide?

9 Write down **three** words that tell us what the lion looked like.

10 a) What did the mother want the dragon to do?
   b) Did the dragon do this?

B

1 How do we know from the story that the mother thought her son was not telling the truth about the lion?

2 a) When the mother gave her son the matchbox do you think she believed there was a dragon inside?
   b) How do we know from the story that the mother thought this way?

3 Why were the boy and the lion able to go and play outside?

4 a) Do you think there really was a dragon?
   b) Explain why you think there was, or wasn't, a dragon.

C

The lion says 'Some stories are true, and some aren't...' **Plan** a story that you would like to come true.

1 Start by **listing** the characters – don't have more than 3.

2 Decide **where** the story will take place.

3 Make **notes** about what they look like and what they are interested in.

4 Decide **what** you want to come true.

5 Write down **how** your wish will come true.

Now write the story!

New ideas from the East

This page is from a history book. It explains how when European knights returned from fighting in the crusades against the Muslims they brought back with them many of the ideas, inventions, foods, fabrics, furnishings and skills they had found in the Islamic world.

In spite of themselves, some of the Christians had to admire the way the Muslims lived. The crusaders copied these ways and took them back to Europe. They brought back the carpets and wall hangings of the East and put them in their castles. A few improved their table manners. They stopped using their fingers and began to use forks as the Arabs did. They learned to use spices, such as pepper, with their food. This was to become very important later.

As trade improved between East and West, other new ideas appeared in Europe. Not all of them had been thought up by Arabs or Turks. Quite often they had just been passed on from places like India and China. They included better ways of sailing, telling the time and working out sums.

Our own numbers are based on those the Arabs copied from India. It was much easier for merchants to keep their accounts with the new figures. All the same, the new system didn't catch on straightaway. The old Roman letters hung on for centuries and are not completely dead even now. Do we not still write 'Henry VIII' rather than 'Henry 8'?

jewellery

rock crystal

perfume

astrolabe

mirror

cloves

glass

enamel

rice

ginger

nutmeg

porcelain

almonds

Arabic numerals

The questions in section A are about the text.

1 In which part of the world did the crusaders live?

2 Before they went to Muslim countries what did the crusaders eat with?

3 Why were the Arabs not such messy eaters as the crusaders?

4 Why was Arab food tastier than the food the crusaders were used to?

5 Name **two** countries from which the Turks and Arabs got some of their ideas.

6 The number nine can be written like this: **IX**. What is the proper name for this type of numbers?

The questions in section B are about the picture and the labels. All the things that have labels in the picture were used first by the Muslims then copied by the crusaders.

1 a) Look carefully at the two long strips of paper with Arabic numerals on them. Write down **two** numbers that are **exactly** the same as the ones you use today in your maths.

b) Write down a number that is a back-to-front version of a number you use.

2 Name **one** food the crusaders found the Muslims were using.

3 List **three** different materials the Muslims made containers from.

4 Why did the Muslims find it easier than the crusaders to take specks of sand out of their eyes?

A crusader comes back from the East. He brings all the things you can see in the picture with him. He decides to invite a great many people to a welcome home party. His special guests are his mother, his brother who loves good food, his sister who has a pet monkey, his uncle who loves wine, and his cousin who lent him the money to buy his armour.

1 Make a **list** showing which present he will give to each of his special guests.

2 Write a card to each of his special guests, saying why he wants to give them this particular present.

Christopher Columbus

These two pages are from an information book on explorers.

Christopher Columbus (c. 1451–1506)

Christopher Columbus came from Genoa in Italy. He believed that he could sail across the Atlantic Ocean and reach the East Indies near China. No one would listen to him except Queen Isabella of Spain. She gave him three small ships, the *Pinta*, the *Nina* and the *Santa Maria*.

1 Which **country** was Columbus born in?

2 Which **town** was Columbus born in?

3 Which powerful person helped Columbus?

4 Which ocean was Columbus going to sail across?

5 Which part of the world was Columbus trying to reach?

6 a) Look at the picture. Which one of the people in the picture do you think is Columbus?

b) Why do you think this person is Columbus?

In August 1492 he set sail. After two months' sailing, on October 12th he sighted land. He was sure he had reached the East Indies and he returned home delighted. He was mistaken, however, for what he had really found were the West Indies.

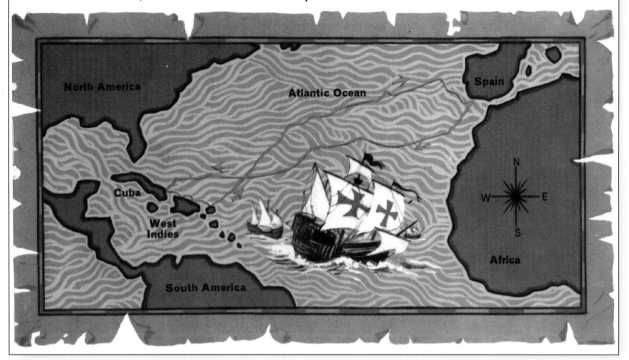

1 How long did the journey take?

2 What was the name of the **first** island Columbus discovered when he sailed away from Spain?

3 **a)** What is the name **we** give to the other islands Columbus discovered?
   b) Where did Columbus think he was?

4 If you look at the map of Africa you will see a **compass** showing which way is North, South, East and West.

   If Columbus had sailed **north** after first sighting land, where would he have ended up?

5 If, when he was coming home, strong winds had blown Columbus to the **east**, where would he have ended up?

Imagine you are on one of Columbus's ships. On October 10th 1492 you have been out of sight of land for two months! Imagine how you feel. There is no way of knowing where you are, there are no radios, nothing! You don't think you will ever see your home again. You decide to put a **message** in a bottle and hope it will float back to Spain. There is only space on the paper for twenty words. What do you write?

Greedy for gold

This page is from a history book, describing what happened after Columbus's exploration. In the sixteenth century soldiers and sailors from Europe made more and more expeditions to the Americas. They met the people who lived there, and sometimes the Europeans made friends with them. But often the Europeans fought them and stole their gold.

The most famous gold in history was in South America. It belonged to the Aztec and Inca people who lived there. But the Spanish went to South America. They wanted to take all the gold for themselves. The Spanish soldiers fought and killed many of the Aztecs and Incas. They sent the gold back to Spain. Then they made the rest of the Aztec and Inca people mine the gold for them. The Spanish became the richest people in all Europe.

The Spaniards plundered and raided the tribes in South America in search of gold treasures.

A

1 Where did these people come from who went to the Americas in the sixteenth century?

2 Why did the explorers fight the people who lived in the Americas?

3 Look at the picture. What did the Aztecs and the Incas make from gold?

4 In which part of the Americas did the Aztecs and the Incas live?

B

1 When the Spanish had taken all the Aztec and Inca gold, what did they do with it?

2 When the Spanish had taken all the gold they could find, what did they make the Aztecs and Incas do next?

3 What happened to Spain after the Spanish soldiers had collected all the gold that belonged to the Aztecs and the Incas?

4 What do **you** think should have happened to the Aztec and Inca gold?

5 Find the word in the picture that means **robbed**.

6 Look at the picture carefully. Why do you think the Spanish won the battles against the Aztecs and the Indians?

C

Imagine you go back in a time machine to when the Spaniards stole the gold that belonged to the Aztecs and the Incas.

You land in the market place of an Aztec town.

You hear an Aztec and a Spaniard giving their different **points of view**.

The Aztec said, 'It's not fair! You Spaniards have taken all our gold!'

The Spaniard laughed, 'It's your fault. You should have made a strong army to guard all the gold.'

'We had no need for armies before you came,' groaned the Aztec.

'I don't believe you! How did you get the gold?' shouted the Spaniard.

The **argument** goes on. Write down what they say next.

The Globe Theatre

This is a page from a history book about Elizabethan times.

The Globe

Many actors travelled around the country performing plays in the open air. Some theatres were built in London. The most famous of these was the Globe, which was built in Southwark in London. It was a round wooden building with an open roof. People came to the Globe and paid to watch plays. Plays were acted from two o'clock in the afternoon until night. There were no women actors, so the women's parts had to be played by young boys.

Shakespeare was one of the owners of the Globe. Many of his plays were performed there. He must have been very upset when, in 1613, the Globe caught fire during a play and was burnt to the ground.

The flag showed that a play was being performed.

Rich people sat in seats in the galleries.

There was a trap-door in the floor. When evil characters in the plays died they pretended to go through the trap-door to hell.

Poor people stood on the ground. They were called 'groundlings'. They often shouted during the plays and threw food at the actors. Shakespeare teased them by writing about the 'groundlings' in his plays.

1 In which city was the Globe Theatre?

2 How could you tell from **outside** the Globe that a play was taking place?

3 During which part of the day were the plays acted at the Globe?

4 What happened to the **groundlings** if it started to rain?

5 What sort of writing was Shakespeare famous for?

6 Look at the picture carefully. Why do you think the Globe burnt so easily when it caught fire in 1613?

1 Why would a **groundling** have to have strong legs?

2 What did the **groundlings** do if the play was badly acted?

3 Give **two** reasons why the rich people had a more comfortable time at the Globe compared to the groundlings.

4 What unusual job did boys do at the Globe?

5 Why do you think the Globe was built in a circular shape?

6 Would you prefer:
   a) to go back in time and see a play at the Globe?
   b) to see a play in a modern theatre?

   Why did you make this choice?

When you are making a **play** you have to write down the words that the different people in your story would say to each other.

Write a **play** about the fire in 1613 when the Globe burnt down.

One of the people in your play can be a **rich woman** sitting in the top gallery. She sees the fire start in the thatched roof. What does she say?

Another person in your play can be a **groundling**. The groundling hears the rich woman shout and tries to escape! What does the groundling say?

The third person in your play can be a **boy actor**. He is on the stage. He tries to help the people in the audience to reach safety. What will he say?

The trees and the axe

This is one of Aesop's fables, retold in modern language.

The trees and the axe

Once a man wanted to cut down
some trees to make a house,
but he could not use his axe
because it had no handle.

So he went to the top of a hill
where there were many trees
and said to them,
"May I take a tree from this hill?"

But he did not tell them why.

The trees said to one another,
"Let us give him a very little tree.
Then he will go away
and not ask us for anything more."

So they gave him a little tree
and the man went home.
When he got there
he made a handle for his axe.

Then he went back to the hill and
began to cut down the other trees.

"If we had not let him have
the little tree he could not have cut
us down," they said.

But it was too late
to stop him.

Moral:
*Be careful when you give way over
small things, or you may have to give
way over big ones.*

56

A

1 What did the man want to build his house out of?

2 Why couldn't the man use his axe?

3 Where were the trees growing?

4 What did the trees give the man?

5 What did the man make with the present the trees had given him?

6 What did the man do when he came back to see the trees again?

B

1 Why did the trees give the man what he wanted?

2 What should the trees have done **before** they gave the man what he wanted?

3 Which **one** of these words do you think describes the man best?

    stupid   lazy   cunning   bossy   angry   weak   frightened

4 How has the artist who drew the picture made the trees look as though they could speak?

C

In the story about The Trees and the Axe we learn what the man did, what the trees said and what they felt.

We don't hear much about the little tree.

The little tree is given away by the other trees.

The little tree is changed into something else.

The little tree becomes the man's helper.

Imagine the little tree kept a **diary**. Every day it put in its diary what it did and how it felt.

How do you think the little tree felt when the big trees said the man could take it?

How do you think the little tree felt when the man took it back to the trees in its new shape?

Start like this:

Monday: I was blowing in the wind when a man came up to talk to us.

How dolphins were created

This is a traditional tale, or myth, about why dolphins may have magical powers.

One day Dionysos, the god of wine, set sail from the Greek mainland with a cargo of vines to plant on one of the islands. But before he'd gone very far, pirates ambushed him and threw him and his vines into the ship's hold. They meant to take him to the nearest temple, and collect a fat ransom from the priests for his safe return. But as the ship sailed on its way, vine-shoots began growing from the hold and spreading their green tendrils along the masts and spars until bunches of ripe grapes hung over the ship from stem to stern.

The pirates stormed down to the hold to see what was happening, and found that Dionysos had changed into a lion, baring its teeth and snarling among the vines. Terrified, they dived into the sea – and Dionysos changed back from lion to god. He took pity on the pirates and turned them into dolphins, leaping and diving beside the ship as it sailed on its way. The sea-god Poseidon saw the dolphins and so admired their speed and grace that he asked them to be his personal bodyguard. They have served him as messengers and sea-guides ever afterwards, as sleek and proud as the soldiers who surround a mortal king on land.

A

1 Write down the word that explains what Dionysos was:

boat   pirate   god   dolphin

2 What was Dionysos carrying on his boat?

3 Where was Dionysos going?

4 Why was Dionysos going on this journey?

5 Who interrupted his journey?

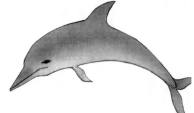

B

1 What was the first sign the pirates had that something was wrong?

2 What did the pirates find when they looked in the hold of the ship?

3 How did the pirates try to escape?

4 What did Dionysos turn the pirates into?

5 What sort of god was Poseidon?

6 Name **two** jobs Poseidon asked the dolphins to do for him.

7 Write down **three** words used in the story that describe parts of the boat.

8 **a)** What would you like to be best of all: a dolphin, a pirate or Dionysos?
  b) Why do you think this choice is the best one to make?

C

1 List all the events in the story that could really have happened. Then list all the events that couldn't be real.

How much of your first list is from the first paragraph? How much of your second list is from the second paragraph?

2 List any words you wouldn't use in your own writing. Look them up in the dictionary, and write down their meanings.

The first Halloween

This story was told to children in Celtic times to warn them about the dangers of being out at night on The Eve of Samhain.

On the Eve of Samhain one year, a handsome stranger came to the village and asked to meet the best harpist in the area, a man named Culag. The stranger offered Culag a bag of gold if he would come and play at a feast. At first Culag refused but a sight of the gold tempted him and at last he went with the stranger to a large hall not far away where there were over a hundred guests. Culag played music for them all night until he became so tired, he fell asleep.

When he awoke the next morning, he found himself lying on the grass at the foot of a little hill near a small lake. He was still clutching his harp and the leather purse he had been given. Alas! There were only stones in it.

As he stumbled to his feet, he caught sight of his reflection in the lake. He was amazed at the face which stared back at him. The skin was wrinkled and both his hair and beard were long, tangled and snow-white. When he got home, he found that thirty years had passed. His wife had died and his children were grown and did not know him.

The story of Culag was told to the children as an awful warning of what could happen on the Eve of Samhain. Memories of the festival of Samhain have come down to us through the ages. Today we know it as Hallowe'en.

By the first of February, the earliest flowers were in bloom and the young lambs were being born. Sheep were very important to the Celts because their wool was needed to make clothes. February the first was called Imbolg. The goddess of the feast was Brigit. People prayed to her and made sacrifices on her altars. By doing this, they were hoping that she would give them large and healthy flocks.

A

1 What did the stranger say he would give Culag if he played his harp?

2 Where did Culag have to go to play his harp?

3 Why did Culag fall asleep?

4 What happened to the gold?

5 How was Culag able to see what had happened to his face?

6 Apart from his face being wrinkled, how else had Culag changed?

7 How long had Culag been asleep?

8 What name do we give to the Eve of Samhain?

9 What is the word used in the story for someone who plays a harp?

10 What do you think is the saddest part of the story of Culag?

B

1 Which of their animals did the Celts think Brigit looked after?

2 Why was this animal so important to the Celts?

3 a) In which month did the Celts make sacrifices to Brigit?
   b) Why did the Celts choose this month to celebrate the goddess Brigit?

4 What did the Celts call the festival during which they prayed to Brigit?

C

Culag wrote a song to tell people how dangerous the Eve of Samhain was. This is all that remains of that song. Copy it down and fill in the gaps.

I was greedy, I wanted g _ _ _,

So I did what I was told.

I took my h _ _ _ to the stranger's h _ _ _,

I pl _ _ _ _ and sang to one and all.

But all my gold just turned to st _ _ _,

I awoke and found myself alone.

Don't be like me, get it right,

Stay inside on S _ _ _ _ _ _ ni _ _ _!

Mulla Nasreddin

Among the Muslims who live in Turkey there are many stories about a famous religious teacher called Mulla Nasreddin. He taught people by telling funny stories. This is one of those stories.

Nasreddin the Doctor

Nasreddin was visiting a sick friend. The friend was rolling about on the bed, clutching his stomach and groaning. The doctor arrived, took one look at Nasreddin's friend, another look under the bed and said, "Stop eating green apples, and you'll be as right as rain in the morning."

That's all he said, and he took his money and left the house. "If it's that easy being a doctor," thought Nasreddin "I must find out how he does it." He ran after the doctor and said, "How did you know it was eating green apples that was wrong with him?"

"Simple," said the doctor. "There was a pile of apple-cores under the bed."

Some time later, Nasreddin was visiting another sick friend. The friend's wife was just about to fetch the doctor when Nasreddin stopped her and said, "It's all right. A mulla's just as good as a doctor. I'll cure him."

He peered under the bed, tut-tutted, then looked the sick man straight in the eye and said, "Stop eating those slippers, and you'll be as right as rain in the morning."

A

1 How many sick friends did Nasreddin visit?

2 Where was the pain of the first sick friend?

3 Who else came to see the first sick man as well as Nasreddin?

4 Why was the first sick man ill?

5 How did the doctor know what had made the first sick man ill?

B

1 Why do you think Nasreddin wants to be a doctor?

2 What do you think the word **mulla** means?

3 Why doesn't Nasreddin let the wife of the sick man fetch the doctor?

4 Why does Nasreddin look under the bed?

5 Write down the **silliest** thing Nasreddin says.

6 Write down the word used on the other page that means **make better.**

C

Here is another story about Nasreddin. Some of the words are missing. Copy out the story using the words underneath to fill in the gaps.

A friend found _____ throwing tiny pieces of _____ all over the floors in his _____ .

'Have you gone _____ ?' asked the friend.

'No. I am frightening away the _____ ,' said Nasreddin.

'But there are no tigers in this _____ ,' said his friend.

'That _____ it is an excellent method!'

> **country   Nasreddin   shows   tigers   bread   house   mad**

Sources

The texts used in this book are extracted from the following full sources, and we are grateful for their permission to reproduce copyright material.

p 4   From *Collins' Storybox* magazine, reproduced by permission of HarperCollins Publishers Limited.

p 6   From *What Makes It Rain?* by Susan Mayes, © Usborne Publishing Ltd 1989, reproduced by permission of Usborne Publishing.

p 8   From *Mushrooms and Toadstools* (Macdonald First Library, 1970), reproduced by permission of Wayland Publishers.

p 10   From *The Incompetent Dragon* by Janice Elliott (Blackie & Son, 1982), text © 1982 Janice Elliott, reproduced by permission of Richard Scott Simon Limited.

p 12   'Mrs Mather' from *Who's Been Sleeping in My Porridge?* by Colin McNaughton © 1990 Colin McNaughton, reproduced by permission of the publisher, Walker Books Ltd.

p 14   From *Masquerade* by Kit Williams (Jonathan Cape, 1979), reproduced by permission of the author.

p 16   From *Amazing Environments* by Terry Jennings (OUP Factfinders, 1995), reproduced by permission of Oxford University Press.

p 18   From *Water* by Alfred Leutscher and Nick Hardcastle, text © 1983 Alfred Leutscher, illustrations © 1983 Nick Hardcastle, reproduced by permission of the publisher, Walker Books Ltd.

p 20   From *The Survival Handbook* by Peter Darman (Headline, 1994), reproduced by permission of Amber Books.

p 22   From *Surrey Heath Official Guide* 1996, based on Ordnance Survey map © Crown copyright 87567M, reproduced by permission of Surrey Heath Borough Council and Ordnance Survey.

p 24   From *The Oxford Illustrated Junior Dictionary*, reproduced by permission of Oxford University Press.

p 26   From *The Oxford Children's Book of Knowledge*, reproduced by permission of Oxford University Press.

p 28   From *Exploring Science* by Roger Hurt (1992), reproduced by permission of Ladybird Books Limited.

p 32   From *The Oxford Children's Book of Knowledge*, reproduced by permission of Oxford University Press.

p 34   From 'Give me 5' (1996), brochure produced by Educational Communications on behalf of Channel 5 Broadcasting Limited, reproduced by permission.

p 38   Two verses of 'The Adventures of Isabel' by Ogden Nash from *Verses from 1929 On* (Little Brown & Co, 1959), Copyright © 1936 by Ogden Nash, renewed, reproduced by permission of Curtis Brown, Ltd. Page illustrated by Mary McQuillan from Michael Harrison and Christopher Stuart Clark (eds): *Oxford Treasury of Classic Poems* (OUP, 1996), reproduced by permission of Oxford University Press.

p 40   From 'Anastasia' by Dennis Manton in *The Loch Ness Monster and Other Mysteries* (Black Cat, 1980).

p 42   From *Razor Rock* by James Webster (Help Yourself, Nelson, 1975), reproduced by permission of Thomas Nelson.

p 44   'Ruby' by Florence Parry Heide from *Tales for the Perfect Child*, Copyright © Florence Parry Heide 1985, reproduced by permission of Piccadilly Press Limited. Page illustrated by Caroline Crossland from Dennis Pepper (ed): *Oxford Funny Story Book* (OUP, 1996), reproduced by permission of Oxford University Press.

p 46   'A Lion in the Meadow' by Margaret Mahy from M Mahy (ed): *Oxford Treasury of Children's Stories* (OUP, 1994), reproduced by permission of Oxford University Press.

p 48   From *Oxford Junior History* Book 2 by Roy Burrell, reproduced by permission of Oxford University Press.

p 50   From *Christopher Columbus: In History – Explorers* by David Smith and Derek Newton (1971), reproduced by permission of Schofield and Sims, Publishers.

p 52   From *The Gold Diggers* by Driscoll and Belinda Hollyer (Macdonald Educational, 1977), reproduced by permission of Wayland Publishers.

p 54   From *Tudor and Stuart Times* by Joan Blyth (Ginn, 1992), reproduced by permission of Ginn & Company.

p 56   Text and illustration for 'The Trees and the Axe' from *A First Book of Aesop's Fables* by Marie Stuart (1974), reproduced by permission of Ladybird Books Limited.

p 58   From *Tales of the Mediterranean: Ancient Greece and Rome*, by Kenneth McLeish (Ginn, 1986), reproduced by permission of Ginn & Company.

p 60   From *Oxford Junior History* Book 1 by Roy Burrell, reproduced by permission of Oxford University Press.

p 62   From *Tales of the Mediterranean: Turkey* by Kenneth McLeish (Ginn, 1986), story based on and adapted from 'Cut Down on your Harness Intake' from *The Exploits of the Incomparable Mulla Nasrudin* by Idries Shah (Octagon Press, London), reproduced by permission of AP Watt Ltd on behalf of JK McLeish and of The Octagon Press Ltd.

Although we have tried to trace and contact all copyright holders before publication this has not always been possible. If notified we will be pleased to rectify any errors or omissions at the earliest opportunity.